This book is to be returned on or before
the last date stamped below

NO...
AND INFORMATION SER...

100% recycled paper

WELDON OWEN PTY LTD

Publisher: Sheena Coupe
Senior Designer: Kylie Mulquin
Editorial Coordinators: Sarah Anderson,
Tracey Gibson
Production Manager: Helen Creeke
Production Assistant: Kylie Lawson

Project Editor: Ariana Klepac
Designer: Patricia Ansell
Text: Jan Stradling

05 04 03 02 01 00
10 9 8 7 6 5 4 3 2 1

Published in New Zealand by Shortland Publications,
2B Cawley Street, Ellerslie, Auckland.
Published in the United Kingdom by
Kingscourt Publishing Limited,
P.O. Box 1427, Freepost, London W6 9BR.
Published in Australia by Shortland-Mimosa,
8 Yarra Street, Hawthorn, Victoria 3122.

Printed in Singapore
ISBN: 0-7699-1257-5

CREDITS AND ACKNOWLEDGMENTS

PICTURE AND ILLUSTRATION CREDITS
[t=top, b=bottom, l=left, r=right, c=centre]
Corel Corporation 10bl, 13tr. **James McKinnon** 3b, 12–13. **Colin Newman** 14b, 15. **PhotoEssentials** banding. **John Richards** 10–11. **Ngaire Sales** 9. **Claudia Saraceni** 6tr, 16. **Kevin Stead** 1c, 3t, 4b, 4–5c, 6tl, 8b, 17.

Weldon Owen would like to thank the following people for their assistance in the production of this book:
Peta Gorman, Michael Hann, Marney Richardson.

Contents

Water Plants   4

Insect Life   6

Frogs   8

Water Birds   10

At Home on the River   12

Where the River Ends   14

Index   16

Water Plants

There are many kinds of plants that live near water. Some plants even live underwater.

Did You Know?

The Amazon water lily is strong enough for a child to sit on.

Duckweed

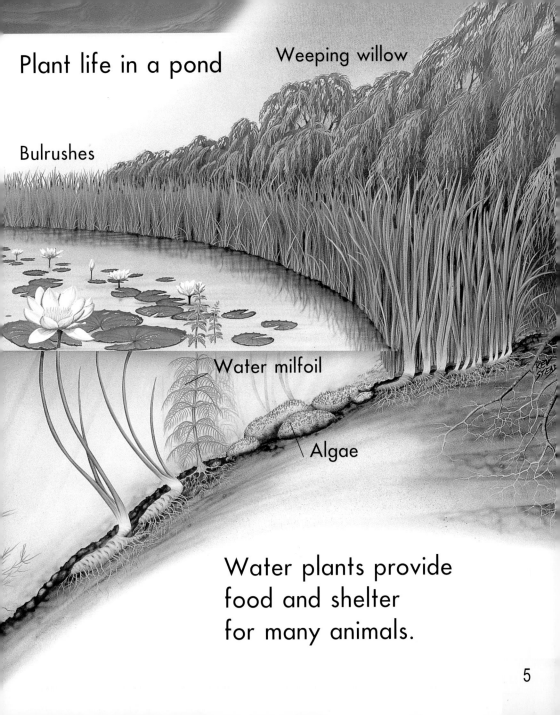

Plant life in a pond

Weeping willow

Bulrushes

Water milfoil

Algae

Water plants provide
food and shelter
for many animals.

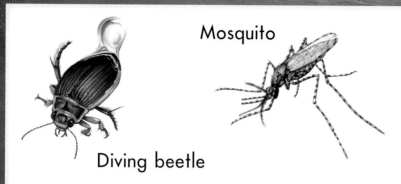

Mosquito

Diving beetle

Insect Life

Many insects live
in fresh water.
Dragonflies begin life
as an egg in a pond.
They like to stay near
ponds and rivers.

1. Female
laying eggs

2. Eggs hatching

The lifecycle of a dragonfly

7. Taking off

6. Climbing out

4. Climbing out of the water

5. Shedding old skin and growing wings

3. Growing into nymphs

Frogs

A frog starts life as an egg in a pond. A tadpole hatches from the egg. The tadpole grows legs. It becomes a frog.

Frogs have strong back legs to help them swim.

The lifecycle of a leopard frog

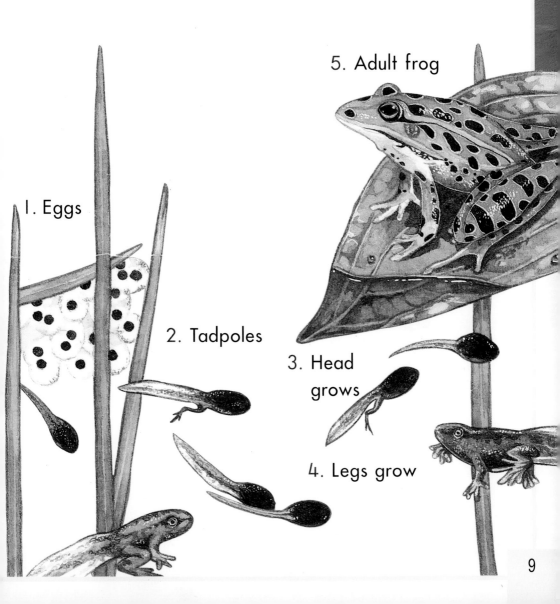

5. Adult frog

1. Eggs

2. Tadpoles

3. Head grows

4. Legs grow

Water Birds

Many birds live near ponds and rivers. There are lots of fish for them to eat. Some birds fly back to the same place every year.

Heron

Egrets

Magpie geese

Stork

Brolga

Jacana

Ducks

At Home on the River

Some animals live on a river.
Beavers chew down trees
and make a dam. Then they make
their home behind the dam.

Young beavers
are called kits.

Dam

Otters live in dens in the banks of rivers, ponds and lakes. The entrance is often underwater.

Underwater doorway

Stone and stick walls

Lodge

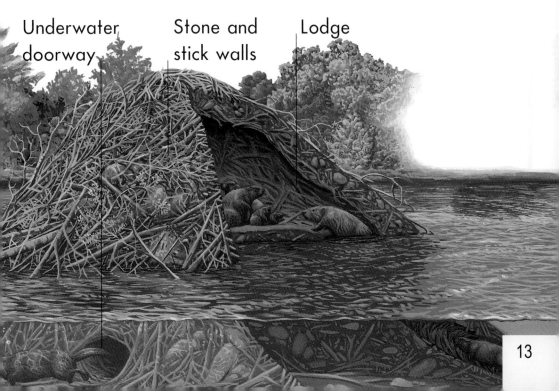

Where the River Ends

All rivers end at the sea. The end of the river is called an estuary. The water is very calm there.

A view from above

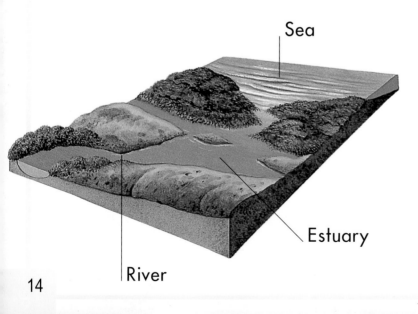

Sea

Estuary

River

An estuary is a good place
for birds and animals
to find food.

Heron

Wading birds

Crab

Fish

Index

beaver   12, 13

birds   10, 11, 15

crab   15

dragonfly   6, 7

estuary   14, 15

fish   10, 15

frogs   8, 9

insects   6, 7

mosquito   6

otter   13

plants   4, 5

river   6, 12, 14

tadpole   8, 9